Death

Marx & Lenin
Ideology

hope for communism
without class society

Death of Marx & Lenin Ideology

hope for communism without class society

Seyed Ali Asghar Emadi Pahandari

Emadi Pahandari, Seyed Ali Asghar

Death of Marx & Lenin Ideology
a Critical Analysis

Published by: Seyed Ali Asghar Emadi Pahandari, Edmonton, Canada

ISBN – paperback: 978-1-77354-253-9

eBook: 978-1-77354-254-6

I DEDICATE THIS BOOK TO MY GOOD PARENTS:
MIR EMAD EMADI PAHANDARI AND SARAH
FARHADI KNOWN AS DEAR MRS. MULUK

Contents

Beginnings: Simple Private Ownership Society

After the collapse of the Russian "Soviet Union" the world announced the death of Communism. In fact, what died were the theories of Marx and Lenin — not communism, because communist is not an idea or theory to die. Historical Materialism and some of the dialectic of Marx were based on metaphysics, not the dialectic.

Marx and Lenin theories were enough to damage the international movement for class society's interest. Instead of communist progress, they propagandized another class society called Socialist. What Marx and Lenin said about socialism is irrelevant because socialism never reached the communist, it does not matter who leads socialism toward communist. Marx made the theory or idea for communists and a theory needs to be practised by a group and this gives power to the group and power brings corruption.

There are many contradictions in Marxism and Leninism. First, Marx and Lenin's ideas were based on metaphysics and their way cannot provide a better life for mankind. Second, class society did not come by revolution and will not go by revolution. Third, communist society is against violence; thus, after the violence, you cannot have a com-

munist society. Peace will not come by the knife as class society believed. In general, their ideas were essentially another
class society which cannot make a significant difference.

Marx's first mistake was he saw primitive ownership
society as a commune. People hunting together and eating
together, for Marx was enough to see the society as common,
not the simple primitive ownership society. Marx thought
the private ownership means having a home, cow, farm, and
money; thus, he could not imagine the private ownership
is the strong man gets a bigger meal, better spot for sit and
sleep, or having more beautiful wives.

Marx's understanding of commune was, when a child
does not have a father in simple primitive ownership society and anyone has intercourse with each other or the man
and woman are nude; thus, he called First Simple Primitive
Ownership society as a commune. He never thought all of
those things may come from lack of knowledge about clothes
or it may came from ignorance. He never thought such a
society was based on some form of simple Private Ownership
society such as the strongest man become a leader; thus, the
strong man first gets his meal. Marx and Lenin understood
communist as very simple and could not figure out important thing happened within the Primitive Ownership Society
which became the first block of class society. Marx did not
understand their way of life forming the government for
future generation.

In Simple Primitive Ownership Society when the strongest man became a leader and other strong man working with
him in hunting they soon had the privilege to get a meal
after the leader. Or the son of the strong man can become a

leader after him. In fact, this kind of stuff in our simple society later became government in our class society. Marx and Lenin did not understand this and they said a Simple Private Society is a commune society.

Based on materialism, progress is toward forward and betterness. I am not sure about it, but I believe it is toward forward, which caused by antagonistic or conflict. Like our time which always forward and never goes backward. Thus, based on materialism we cannot have a commune society and then go to slavery (means from good and no class society goes to class society). This was a mistake Marx made in his theory because he did not understand materialism very well. We lived in a Simple Private Society, not the Commune as Marx mentioned.

Communism was/is every man's desire, but how we can reach such a desirable thing is a question. For example, reaching desirable food for man is to get food he likes; thus, he does not make any idea and all he needs is how to reach the food he likes. Second, Class society has an idea because some group wants to rob the others; thus, the idea provides such an opportunity for them.

Marx made an idea for a man how to reach the Communist and his reasoning pushed him toward metaphysics.

In Historical Materialism, Marx studied every class Society from the Simple Ownership Society "Marx called commune" to capitalism. He concluded that a Capitalist Society is based on the oppression of a man on another man: thus, every man for their survival does anything. All men are alienated and cannot see the truth; thus, in such society, the working class must stand up and lead the revolution toward victory and take society under their wings and lead the society 'Socialism", toward Communism.

What Marx concluded was based on metaphysics and Marx did not study Slavery and Feudalism well; as a result, his conclusion was wrong. Marx did the same as what Spartacus did during slavery. Marx and Lenin made another class society idea and called it Socialism.

Marx spoke of the alienation of the man in class society and it is true, but the problem here is Marx alienated himself from his family and from society. Marx did not pay attention to himself and his family. A person who studied 16 hours a day can not pay attention to his and his family's needs. Two of his children died from starvation and his wife, who was a strong woman and from well known family, suffered a lot from stress and emotional problems because Marx payed more attention to his book than to her. Marx alienated from society because he did not understand communist and capitalism and never figured out what their real differences.

The Socialism of Marx and Lenin is nothing other than another form of class society and it could not eliminate poverty. If socialism is a class society with a big gap between rich and poor, why we do a revolution in capitalism. Second, how is it is possible we have social nationalism, Christian socialism, even social democrat? Or, how are all socialism leaders billionaires? Lenin was Bolshavic leader when he separated from Manshavic in 1905, he did not say to them you can not be a social democrat. As a result, socialism continues toward capitalism because it is a class society and nothing more and it never goes toward communist. The Communist

Party of Iran said: Socialism For Ever means Class Society For Ever.

Marx alienated with the book and he ignored his family. If you study more than a week for 16 hours a day, your mind can not get anything from the material you study; as result, Marx had mental problems because a normal person cannot study every day 16 hours. Marx's idea could not provide a better world and people after him did not identify the mistake which Marx had made and they did the same mistake that Marx did it.

The crime that capitalism committed against Marx is unprecedented. German capitalism exiled Marx although he had a high degree, but capitalism left Marx without a job and without financial aid. Marx's mind was busy from the cruelty of the capitalism system. I think Marx was trying to escape from the cruelty of the capitalism and he was making himself busy by reading and writing. However, his mind could not observe the material he was reading.

Marx talked about a productive worker's surplus-value and by this surplus-value the rich become richer than before. He made the working class lead society toward communist.

My challenge is, to change society, we must change people's minds. Now, this productive worker does not want anything changed. Second, why do only productive workers made surplus value? I believe anyone working in class society can make surplus value. Third, does such surplus value exist in socialism and if exists, where does this surplus-value go?

In the Soviet Union "by many Iranian books" there were many people in Moscow train and bus stations asking people for food and money. If such a thing is socialism, I am saying people do not want such a society.

Class Society

People dream of the society to be free; first from poverty, and later from other chains on their necks. People do not dream to be like beggars because we are not Sofia or Hindu and Janis, We are communists who value all of the human desire and communist society made all human desire happens in reality, not in a dream.

First, we must eliminate poverty, but because socialism it is a class society, socialism could not eliminate poverty. People do not want King Bush or Obama's "Capital" changed to King Castro "Socialism". What people want is a society without poverty and chains.

As socialism was class society; thus, America and other Western Nation or Imperialism tried very hard to use communist as socialism for Soviet, Cuba, China, and others but they had little success to killed people's dream and damaged the communist. Communist will come but not by Marx and Lenin's theory and Communist will come not by some parties or groups who want to lead society. Communism will come when all the people work together and run society together.

Why Marx made such a nasty idea is another question. In my view, Marx may have stolen the idea and used it in the way that capitalism has benefited from it. Fourteen hundred years ago Muhammad the Prophet of Islam chose the Mostazafan as his follower against Abo-Sofian, and Marx maybe thought the working class suffered most from the capitalist society, and chose them to lead socialism toward the communist. But the problem is, forming a government is the biggest major issue that leads Marx toward the metaphysic. Muhammad made government, but that was over 1400 years ago "always remember the time".

Marx and Lenin, especially Lenin, had a kind of personal hate toward Russian imperialism; thus, they were not able to think materialistic. Both of them did not realize everything we have in society came from the class society; as a result, they moved toward metaphysics rather than move toward materialism dialectics. Both could not figure out that communist society is not the idea and communist society wanted to break all ideas which are the chains in human necks.

What I see is a big gap in the history of humanity in the Western nations. In fact, a human may build a strong weapon or go to the moon but with all of this, the human's biggest problem is selfishness and just looking for his/her own interest. For example, Russo, based on his view, saw all human problems based on society and today psychologists see all human problems except suicide related to the individual. Or Darwin said about the evolution and survival of the fittest and capitalism used for centuries to deceive the people of the third world countries. I want to say, Western nations for their interest used different ways to put some of their people and put third "undeveloped" nations to sleep. Unfortunately, Marxism and Leninism were other things that Western Nations bought and used for their present and future interest.

Marx and Lenin were dualists because they acted as dualism about religion. They did it because the class society wants them to do it. From 13 century free-mason began in Scotland, England and possibly Italy. Free-mason is atheism and they do not believe religion and you must be homosexual to become a member of this idiot upper class in Western nations club or whatever you want to call it. Catholics before the 18 century fought with this idea but after the 18 century accepted the dirt and become part of the free-masons.

After the 19 century many Western politicians and people in Western nations, and other countries are part of the free-mason today. In fact, after the 15 century (the beginning of capitalism) the upper class does not see the religions as profitable things for their class societies. Vatican (the Vatican became a country during Napoléon by Napoleon) is just a symbol of the past and nothing more for Western Politicians and many people of the Western nations. Most Popes belong to free-mason and if one of them does not belong to free-mason he cannot do anything because he is just a symbol and nothing more. Marx consciously or unconsciously acted for benefits of the class society but Lenin was a puppet and finished what the Western nation could not do.

Dualism and Hypocrisy

In my opinion, an educated person must do the research and must find out why Moses, Jesus (it does not matter if they are real or a myth) and Muhammad came and what message they had. Marx acted most personally toward Jewish and Christianity and he did not understand or he did not do any research toward religions. Marx wrote a few things about Jewish and Christianity. For example, he wrote about Christianity, "Jesus advocated helping the poor, but the Christian church merged with the oppressive Roman state, taking part in the enslavement of people for centuries. In the Middle Ages, the Catholic Church preached about heaven but acquired as much property and power as possible."

Lenin acted in dualism in other areas. For example, in 1905 he said we are not the Menshevik anymore because we are not the social democrat and we are the communist. But he later wrote, "you must be socialism or capitalism". Also, Lenin said socialism is not the society and it is just a way from capitalism (or imperialism) toward communism. However, Lenin said socialism is the way but he mentions you must be socialism or capitalism, not the communist. He also said the working class and upper class (bourgeois) are stable and middle class is not. Marx and Engels in Historical Materialism actually expressed ideas that were based on metaphysics rather than materialism.

Marx mentioned another form of the government in the hand of the working class and he called it the first Fuzz of Communism. Also, he said the government's job is the oppression of the other class. As a result, if the working class forms the government, its job is to oppress other classes. Lenin did not trust the illiterate working-class and he said "how one laundrywoman knows about politics and we take the government and teach them how to run the system than we put the government in working-class hand."

Lenin believed that until the working class learned the politic this will be our responsibility to lead socialism toward communist. First, Lenin did not eliminate poverty in the Soviet Union when Lenin and others had power. Second, they never give the power to the working class because they become a bureaucrat. Third, no class learns how to run government unless in education increases among all classes, and such a thing never happened during Lenin.

Lenin was a hypocrite and created the NEP (Lenin New Economic Policy- 1922). Lenin came to terms with the great landlords and said that he would deal with them later, was two steps forward and one step backward. In fact, the NEP proved socialism was a class society and lost to capitalism or imperialism and as we saw in 1989 with its collapse.

Stalin tried hard to save Marx and Lenin's ideas. He made one million working classes as members of the socialist political party "such as Nikita Khrushchev". As they never expected, the Working class in socialism political party become bureaucrats, and they started to use their power toward other working class in the Soviet and even abused their power toward anyone who opposed their way.

Marx chose the working class to get support from another class who does not have any education. Marx said any class in power oppressed the other classes, but he still chose the working class as a leading class. Marx maybe thought, the worker was always oppressed by the upper class and middle class and never thought the working class in a short process will become bureaucrat or become an upper class and oppressed working class or oppressed other classes.

What we want is to end the class society and to end oppression. For example, you made a society with two classes; one by the upper class and second with the working class. The upper class oppress the working class and no class or anyone does not have means and the second class is working-class oppressed upper class and no class or finally, working-class or anyone does not have means. As you see, both classes are the same but one you call Capitalism or Imperialism and the other one you call Socialism.

Who was Marx? I said something before about him but that was no answer. Communism was the hope and dream of an oppressed people but always it was just hoped until Marx. If he stole the idea or not is no big deal, but he tried to bring it to reality; however, Marx went the wrong way but his action to make communist as real, is admirable. Capitalism, Imperialism and their puppets always spread that communist is vain imagination and you cannot build it in reality and Marx for first time punched their face and said communist is not imaginative and it is real. Marx attacked on capitalism and metaphysics. But his punch was not in the right spot to knock them down, and again class society believes that communist is a fantasy and communist is death.

Marx and others saw class society as very simple, not complex, and they never thought when humans lived in a cave until now made class society very strong.

I mentioned communist society is different from primitive, slavery, feudalism, capitalism or imperialism, and socialism societies and whatever societies there were. These societies were parts of class society. In class society, there is a gap between people: one who has means and the other one has not. Communism is a society without any idea or theory with out poverty and with out any chain in human neck; as a result, it is society different from class societies. Marx sees communist society like imperialism or capitalism; thus, he made an idea or theory for a communist society. When someone made an idea, it means other people must get the power to put the idea in practice; thus, a communist society is not an idea and does not need any single person or a groups of people to put the idea in practice.

What takes Lenin's neck under the guillotine is that Lenin considered political power as necessary to go toward communist. The reality is, communists want to break the power and everybody be equal and what the Lenin said was another Jung and nothing more.

We know power brings corruption and it does not

matter who has such power. Lenin was the biggest hypocrite. Let me tell you another hypocrisy: He said we must first establish socialism then lead socialism toward communist. The same thing Marx said in Program Geta and Marx said this society must be led by the working class. This is hypocrisy because before the Lenin "Elite" led socialism to communist "never happened" the Elite is too corrupt to give society to the working class and lead socialism toward communist.

Toward a Better Society

Establishing another class society does not lead you any-where and you need another revolution to overthrow this class society. There are many contradictions in both of them. First, class society did not come by revolution and will not go by revolution. Second, communist society is against vio-lence; thus, after the violence, you cannot have a communist society and peace will not come by the knife as class society believed it. War will be with war and if it brings peace just for a short period and what we want is the end of the war and end of the class society and peace, relaxation forever.

As a result, we do not need a revolution and third; we do not need another class society led by any class. We do not need any revolution because we stick to it and it goes on, and goes and we never have any better society because the revolution will bring another revolution and it goes on until the end. Again we do not need to be led by any class because you need another revolution to take power from it; as a result, we are back to my previous point in that we are stuck in revolution until the end. Revolution and violence, is a troubled world.

Another thing that stems from violence is the dictatorship of the proletariat, and Marx has developed it several times in the ghetto program. Some groups believe if we used the democracy of proletariat there will not be any dictatorship. The reality says something else, because when they form government any class society government tries to eliminate its enemies. Second, changing a word in another ways may have a different outcome "not for benefits of the whole society" and it is class society talk. We want all the symbols of class society to disappear from society and this needs time.

One thing that put left and social democrat necks under the axe is that: based on materialism your conflict changed as you changed. For example, when you are the working class you have a conflict with those who have means. When your situation changed and you have means to become upper class your conflict is working class and middle class and no-class. When social democrat says we go and become part of the system and changed the class society to the communist is a lie because when they reach to upper class their conflict is going to change and they will not be communist anymore.

If you tells Mr. Clinton to accept communist society and everybody in America be equal, she will not accept it because she is not the communist anymore. She is the same as Lenin who said we need power and to establish socialism and then take you to a communist society gradually. As a result, when Lenin becomes upper class his desire to change the system becomes zero and, he is against people who do not have any means.

Marx by saying, the working class gets power, he does not know that the working class changed to the upper class and their desire changed for a communist society to go to zero because of their wealth. Same as Lenin who got the power with other middle class, their desire for change goes to zero. Social democrat who believed go to system and become part of the system and by reform changed the negative of class society to positive or the communist. They will not be reformist, as they are not.

They will not be communist after they become an upper class. Again Lenin who took power from the working class will never return to the working class because he become upper class and his desire for communist society becomes zero. This was the reason they did not open the organization to help those who have more children or who need more income for their daily life. Both Lenin and Stalin's desire changed from communist society to class society rather than reaching the communist.

Marx talked about division and its result. In Marx's opinion, people must not be divided because they lose their power. Marx mentioned men and women will become equal when poverty disappears. Marx said it is a possible that in capitalism women may become more powerful than men, but equality will come when poverty disappears. Marx mentioned capitalism desires to divide everything. But the sad thing is the first division was done by the left which was the working class day. Now we can see many, many of these kinds of the division; such many woman rights day, father and mother days, homosexual "gay pride day", teacher day, farmer day, and days for many others. These divisions only separated all humans from any action. I am saying, left did it because it is a class society and nothing more and it shows to capitalism how to decrease people's power.

Marx and Lenin saw the Pope, Bishops, and another religious figures like Moses, Jesus, and Muhammad and acted
against them; as a result they became dualist. What Moses
and Jesus did during their times are different from what
represents the class society Reba, and Pope were/are doing.
The Ten Commandments were a masterpiece of Moses and
people will not follow Ten Commandments as Moses said.
Many Jewish people have problems with this and it seems
it is impossible to follow them. Moses' realization was society like communists, not the class society. In class society,
you can not follow Ten Commandments. He tried to teach
people and to make them ready for a communist society.
Unfortunately, it was too soon for people to accept a better
society.

Later Jesus came and taught people how to share material and how to live peacefully with each other. As time
was not ready for such society; thus, people were blind or
like death could not see or hear what Jesus said. Later class
society changed and made religious leaders as puppets of the
class society.

Then Muhammad came with a different method and
defeated Abu-Sofian and established society and he knows
the time for communist society was soon but in his lifetime,
he tried to teach people to be a better human by brush-
ing their teeth, be clean, and search for the knowledge.
Muhammad read Moses and Jesus' teaching and he realized
how class society put two great men down; as a result, he
said I do not have a miracle and my only miracle is my book.
Muhammad knew what a monster class society is and how
they motivated people to do things and the people will do

it; thus, Muhammad increased his teaching. He chose Ali after him, but Abu-Baker, Omar, and Othman came first. Unfortunately, when Ali came, because of the many enemies he had, he become too conservative to change the people toward better living.

Moses, Jesus, and Muhammad were not, metaphysic and they were materialism. They are materialism because they act to save their people. On the other hand, Marx, Lenin, Mao, and others went toward dualism. Based on their ideas they become good and religion becomes bad. Definitely, the future will talk about them more because Moses, Jesus and Muhammad are part of our history.

Capitalism or class society did not leave Marx alone. As mentioned after many thousands of years class society has tremendous experience; thus, he used this experience for a long life of the class society. The class society knows that materialism with a strong weapon (truth) very soon can stand up against class society and metaphysics. Western class society upper-class were atheism. During the 13 century they established Freemason; as a result, they bring Moses and Jesus down well. Catholic until the 18 century still believed the Jesus; however, their teaching was against Jesus. After the 18th century the Pope and most of the upper-class Catholics become Freemason. This means they do not agree with Jesus and they only believed there must be God in the universe. As they know materialism will come, but they found one of the wealthy person, Engles, to become friends with Marx and damaged materialism.

Now lefts and rights are working together for the long life of the class society; who can deny this? The class society of Marx, Lenin and Mao give new life to imperialism and class society imperialism. Now the future belongs to another class society which is socialism. How and what class society had done to Marx theory? First, Marx was dogmatic and he believed he was the rightist man in the world. Second, they made friends for him and it was Engels who helped Marx financially. Third, Engels used his financial ability to damage Marx and Marx's theory very well.

The oppressed person during Prophet Muhammad did not belong to any class and it belongs to all the class. In fact, they are people who are more bitten by a chain on their back. Class society may oppress the working class but that does not mean the working class, as a class can lead society. First, other people are more oppressed than the working class.

Time is an important factor. Prophet Muhammad lived in his time but he acted much better than Marx who lived in capitalist time. Marx and Lenin thought they can change the social structure of society without changing people's mind first. Marx and Lenin thought they can control social structure without help from people. If Marx and Lenin had a different implementation and worked to change people's minds then automatically the social structure of the society would change because people do not want oppression and class and they do not satisfy people's needs.

Socialist Economics

Socialist economics refers to the economic theories, practices, and norms of hypothetical and existing socialist economic systems. A socialist economic system is characterized by social ownership and operation of the means of production that may take the form of autonomous cooperatives or direct public ownership.

Public ownership can not create such a big gap between rich and poor. In fact, there must not be any gap if socialism really wants to go toward communist. Poverty must be eliminated without public ownership economic system.

The economic system is designated as a socialist planned economy. Non-market forms of socialism usually include a system of accounting based on calculation-in-kind to value resources and goods.

As all chains of class society are broken, no one leader or any kind of authority rules, no one says anything to anyone and everyone does their job well "all of these are part of public ownership"; thus, it is a communist society based on public or social ownership. Lenin sees socialism as a way toward communist. Second, how you want to do public ownership when all the people have a capitalist mind and

few people take power in their hands and they won't lead socialism toward communist. There is poverty by public ownership. Communism is social ownership without any person or
groups leading it or controlling it. But socialism is class society as Lenin in the New Economic Policy used Free Market
and Mixed Economic system.

I am not going to talked about the Central Planing
System but I would like to say a few things. The class society
or class society tradition has always put different kinds of
the economic systems that may have been acceptable to that
period of the time. They compare one with another and say
which economic system is good or bad. But their economic
decision making system never shows it works for the benefits
of the whole people, not for benefits of a few authorities.

Government gives the power to a group and such power
makes the group corrupt. it does not matter who that group
is: The production of goods and services in command econ-
omies is often done by state-owned enterprises, which are
government owned companies. In centrally planned econ-
omies, which are sometimes referred to as "command econ-
omies", prices are controlled by bureaucrats.

The problem of Marx and others was they did not know
what materialism is and how to be materialism; and second,
they were completely blind as to what communist is. They
thought scientific thinking is materialist thinking. Marx,
Lenin and others saw class society problems as based on religion and religious philosophy. Even Marx was against capitalism but he was not against atheism. We know many Western
Nations in politics are atheist and they defended class society
very well. Marx could not be a supporter of Moses because

he was against religion. Marx did not have time to analyze everything that class society is using, everything in society for class society benefits. As a result, they used religion too, and still, they are using religion as a symbol.

Vision is an important factor, and both Marx and Lenin did not see farther than their own time. People who do not go a little be farther than their own time cannot be "genius". Lenin was primarily concerned with political power to go toward communist. All negative things we have, came from political power; and political power never gives anything right except to be in power or have means in your hands. This man didn't reckon with the fact political power does not go to the communist, only society after the death of political power goes toward communist.

Marx prescribed social ownership for First Fuzz but he agrees the working class must lead it to the communist. Marx didn't figure out that the working class does not have the power to take First Fuz toward a communist society. Not only the working class cannot do it, but in my view, no class or groups are able to because we made government and government is power and its job is to oppress others. We need to bring class down by reform so that society is able to go toward communist.

People First

During October 1917, or Lenin time, Russians were not ready for communist; thus, establishing socialism was the wrong move. Even if Lenin could go toward direct social ownership and nobody ran the society and everybody does his/her responsibility at that time, but Russia and its people were not ready for such a big task. People must reach this level where they say why is our country run by a Liberal or Conservative or New Democratic party, Socialist party and we do not need them. If people continue to say, we do not need anyone to control us, why do we let them do that, when we know everybody in society must be equal why do we let some groups cause inequality in society. Again they say, all the hunger, stealing, lies, and social problems are caused by a few people who want to have all the wealth in their hands. Why do we obey them?

Then send their voice to all the world would be "from people, not from a political party". For example, they send their message to others by saying, the earth belongs to everyone, why should a few be rich, and most of us not; why do we have so many social problems and so on? At such a point society may be ready for a better world or communist. In

October 1917 the Russian people and its working-class were thinking so backward rather than looking for a better world. One bourgeois writer said when a nation does not deserve democracy, it will never reach democracy.

Russian people at that time, and even their politicians, were thinking about how they can become rich, rather then building an equal society for everyone. Our goal is to end class society not open another one. I am trying to show many ways to let you know how society from capitalism or imperialism and socialism may go toward the communist.

Marx spoke about conflict and based on conflict we must go toward the level of communists which is achievable. If we go by anti-peaceful conflict, we may be stuck in violence forever, because communist belongs to peaceful conflict. In anti-peaceful conflict we will never end up with a better society – a society without violence, a society that each member respects other members. How could we reach such a society with anti-peaceful conflict? What Marx and Lenin prescribed for the better world was much worse and we never ended in such a society. What they prescribed was another class society which belongs to upper-class people — not belongs to all mankind.

We must go by peaceful conflict toward communist. Marx believed we left the commune toward private ownership, and he was wrong because a society Marx saw as commune was in fact a simple primitive ownership society. Based on materialism, society goes forward, not backward. We started from Simple Private ownership and are still in private ownership. Like moving from one cell to a complex cell, our society started from simple ownership and it goes to the highest complex level. Then our society moves to another level which is not class society nor communist until we reach the communist. The same thing happened to our minds. Marx may think the animals or some primitive culture is/ was living in a commune society. This was a big mistake, and he went toward metaphysics.

Marx, Lenin, Mao, and many other hypocrites were not truly communist because they never figured out when we reach perfection, we will reach communist. Reaching perfection means to break all chains around our neck and become humans who will not lie, steal, and kill; and then we will live in complete freedom.

Freedom and Rights

Many times I mentioned how we can reach communist. Lenin, this Witch of East Wood (movie's name) did not give free expression or free speech. Someone asked Lenin if a priest wanted to be our member, what he must do? Lenin said in the communist party he must not talk about his belief or say anything against the communist party. Why, Mr. Lenin, does he not only have the right to talk about his belief system but also to criticize the communist party?

We see Lenin's opinion about democracy and socialism is much more restrictive than the bourgeois-democratic was. We cannot by force keep people silent and not talk about their beliefs. People must understand and believe and live in freedom. Marx and Lenin made a class society with 100% dictatorship and by such dictatorship tried to run society in the name of building a better society and say they are going toward communist.

Marx and Lenin did not talk about individual rights because they did not know what is the communist. Individual rights in fact is the freedom that does not exist in any class society.

Lenin was against individual rights; thus, the Soviets

closed its door to all the people in the world; also the Soviet people can not see the other countries. This is a reason John Lenin said in the Forrest Gump movie there is not a rich person in China. Infect, there is big gap in China and few are very rich and many are very poor.

China opened its door to the world and its people but it does not mean it has an individual rights because China is a a class society. Class society does not have any individual rights. The Rest of the world does not have any individual right because they are class societies.

Individual Right means any individual do not have political, cultural, social chains or problems on their neck. When a person in a society is hungry, or he wants to have a computer, mobile, or car and he can not get, it means that individual does not have any rights.

Many Left groups (not the communist) I call them left because they accidentally sit on the left side – in fact they are right groups and socialism is class society as capitalism" called Western Nations imperialism have individual rights and they were wrong. There are not any individual rights in Western Nation imperialism or in any class society. In the class society who has money or means has the limited individual right and rest nothing. If the left or someone thinks there is an individual right, I must say that right does not exist, and the whole thing is just an illusion, not the individual right. Individual rights only exist in the society with out any social, material problems and it exists in communist society. What really exists in Western nations, or all class societies, is individualism not individual rights.

When a child born he or she has the same right as an

adult has. Thus, any individual has the right to spent his/her life in any way he/she likes it. He/she is not dependent on anyone and his desire came to reality not just for him but for anyone in the society which we will call earth. Moses, Jesus, and Muhammad want to tell the people that God created the earth for all of you and those have meant more than you, just stole from you. People did not understand them and still, they can not understand communist.

Lenin had a fight with Anarchism and he said some meaningless things. Lenin said the working class and bourgeois are stable and the middle class is unstable and cannot take society toward communist. However, later Lenin doubted about his saying and said the working-class are puppets of the upper class and are a lumpen worker. Still, Lenin was dualism in this area. In my view, all humans are not stable until all of them to reach the level that throws out their benefits in the class society. In communists, all of them have the same benefit.

The mistake Marx did on dialectic: I must say, the universe has a beginning and end. If based on scientists, our universe started by a big bang and is still expanding until one day it may be destroyed by a Black Hole. My question is based on dialectic: life is progressing toward better, and this is the law of our universe. Now, what happens if the earth is destroyed by an asteroid, by the sun, by disasters or by a Black Hole, or the whole universe is destroyed by a Black Hole, what will be? Are we going toward better or worse? I do not think we are progressing toward better. Materialism is not a theory but it is truth. Based on our universe, society or anything goes forward but not toward better.

The universe includes our earth and how the essential items are related to each other. As our knowledge about the universe was few; thus, Materialism Dialectic was not completed. We know that for having a better life, environment for ourselves and all beings, we must not be against the universe as Metaphysics says. We know everything in the universe has begun and will end. We know our universe is expanding and there is not any centre in our universe. We know we came from one cell and the first creature on earth was small then replaced with a bigger one. We know everything our scientists said about the universe and about the earth is a hypothesis and it could be wrong like Galileo or all of them could be right or some of them be right. However, there is not any choice, with little better understanding of the universe and earth we can use materialism dialectic, not the metaphysics.

When I mentioned the first part of the materialism dialectic is irrelevant is the same as one of my old friends told me a long time ago; and his name is Dr. S. S. He was right because mind and body both work together for us and how can we say the body is superior to the mind or vice-versa. We do not know many questions and we do not have an answer for them. For example; does intelligence exist in the big rock who we called earth? Or, is intelligence existing in our universe? If we answered this question positively, we can never say everything happened by accident.

We know all beings on earth have a brain and they are very smart; it is not possible our earth during 4.9 billion years ago, everything happened to earth or everything earth did was based on its intelligence, not that it happened by itself or by accident. Our knowledge about the earth and the universe is very little and we are living in the earth full of wonder and in front of us is a big universe with millions or billions of light-years distance. I said our knowledge about our earth and the universe is so little, if it was not we are not in class society.

God who said human is a superior being, right now God's mind changed and God finds out what a mess he created by choosing humans as the superior being. Human must be compatible with the environment "with peaceful conflict". Our planet is in a critical situation and many animals have disappeared because of human environmental and anti-peaceful behaviour. It seems the earth it going to be changed to a new being.

Many wealthy people who have means still are living in idiocy and others by any means are trying to become like them. If humans will survive, we are going to need to change our mind to live better and show more care for the earth and all the animals and plants.

If a man tries to protect his benefit and say homosexual people have right just like others but they had more right before than now. Now only wealthy gay and lesbian have rights and the rest are living on welfare or living in poor environment. Those wealthy gay and lesbian support of the system is going by metaphysics and they are saying they are supporting the homosexual right and environment right but their philosophy is destroying everything. These people are hypocrites. Our planet is undergoing such transformation and we may not be here anymore. Man tries to protect himself "freemason" and go by metaphysical philosophy, our nature will be destroyed.

I mentioned Marx mistakes such as simple primitive society that he called commune, and I said that Marx instead of establishing communist established another class society named socialism. I said that Marx was so wrong in that he chose the working class because he thought the working class were capable to lead people toward communist and also I mentioned no class has such ability to lead anyone toward communist.

I said communist is not a theory or idea, and Marx made the theory of communist; thus, some people must be a leader to practice Marx's theory in society. Again Marx made a class society instead of communist. Marx mentioned dialectic and Marx in practice was metaphysic. I did not say anything about Mao because he said you must be Buddhist then become communist. I found Mao knew nothing about communist and materialism.

I said about mind and body; however, they are working together, but I said no one preferred body without mind. This is a mistake in some parts of the materialistic; it does not mean that metaphysic is better than materialistic. The universe will go by materialistic.

The books I used in my book are: Contemporary History, Collection of Lenin's work, Collection of Stalin, Mao Red Book, Program of Gotha. I hope the future generation will very soon will realize if they move the Marx, Lenin way, they will never reach the communist.

The future will be better judged. I mentioned how Marx, Lenin, and others went toward metaphysic rather than stayed in materialism; as a result, socialism or fake communist is a class society. Both class are the same.

For example, Fidel Castro had over 1 billion dollars. Mr. Trump has 1.4 billion dollars but China's leader has over 5 billion dollars and is one of the richest people in the world. The North Koran leader "Over 5 billion dollars". The North Korean leader's father who said America is an empty drum "I think" had 4 billion dollars. These left groups do not want to build a better world — they just wanted to be in power instead of imperialism or capitalism. They want to be in power and be rich and call them communists. These people don't think of the many poor people in Cuba or North Korea, China, and other socialist countries.

What I say about all these hypocrites is that they just hate America without building a better society for their people. These hypocrites scream against capitalism or imperialism not building a better world. When asked about themselves, they say you cannot build a better world in one night and we need time.

These were crimes that Marx, Lenin, Mao, and others did to human society. What Marx and Lenin made was class society. Both were like capitalism. Marx named simple private ownership society as commune. He made government and his government must lead by the working class. Marx made an idea or theory for the communist which must be run by the working class. Lenin's idea or theory was run by an elite because he said the working class do not have knowledge to run the society. What these two men made is hard to swallow. Communist is not an idea and nobody can run a communist society. In the end no political parties, organizations or groups in any form have the ability to build a better world and what they do, is work for their own benefit and their parties benefits.

End

Glossary of terms

Simple Private Ownership society "or commune of the Marx": A society that existed before Slavery.

Slavery: A human owned another human legally as Slave. Slave was considered as the property of a man. Slave had no rights and no law which are held by free man.

Feudalism: Most feudal masters were chosen by the king or were known by a king. In Britain they called feudal a Lord and in Iran called feudal a Khan. The Lord or Khan had land and peasants work on Lord or Khan land for very small product of land and military protection or just protection.

Capitalism: Trade and industry are controlled by private ownership for profit.

Socialism: By Lenin it is way toward communist; as result it had both system symbol: One is capitalism and then replaced by communist. and I proved socialism is like other class society only looking for profit can replaced communist symbol and the working class cannot lead socialism toward communist.

Imperialism: Another class society which beside looking for profits, want to extend policy of the country and influence through diplomacy and military.

Communist: people are living without any class society problems. Everything in society is divided based on people's need. Everybody respects each other's rights and people do not lie, steal or murder anyone. Many other issues we can not think about it because we may not reach to communist in 500 or even more years.

Public Ownership Society: Everything in the society belongs to everyone and everyone uses them equally. What Marx or Lenin said about Public Ownership in socialism is Elite Ownership and not public ownership. This is why none of the socialism countries were able to eliminate poverty.

Dictatorial Proletariat: In Marxist philosophy, the dictatorship of the proletariat is a state of affairs in which the proletariat holds political power. The dictatorship of the proletariat is the intermediate stage between a capitalist economy and a communist economy.

Central Planning System: A centrally planned economy, also known as a command economy, is an economic system in which a central authority, such as a government, makes economic decisions regarding the manufacturing and the distribution of products.

Atheism: Atheism is a rejection of any deities. In a narrower sense, atheism is the position that there are no deities.

Materialism: the material world, perceptible to the senses, has objective reality independent of mind or spirit. Materialists did not deny the reality of mental or spiritual processes but affirm that ideas could arise, therefore, only as products and reflections of material conditions.

Dialectic: Everything is in continual process of becoming and ceasing to be, in which nothing is permanent but everything changes and is eventually superseded.

Materialist History: Marx in his historical materialist classified human society to Simple ownership society "by Marx Commune", Slavery, Feudalism, Capitalism.

Peaceful Conflict: It is like man and woman who have peaceful conflict and their outcome "synthesis" is a child which It causes human survival.

Anti Peaceful Conflict: It is like death and living in which death prevails.

Metaphysic: Believed reality existed. It is believed there is no valid set of empirical observations, nor a valid set of logical arguments, which could definitively prove metaphysical statements to be true or false. It is believed, the change in matter or anything is not related to conflict.

Buddhism: A religion, originated in India by Buddha and later spreading to China, Burma, Japan, Tibet, and parts of southeast Asia, holding that life is full of suffering caused by desire and that the way to end this suffering is through enlightenment.

Hinduism: This Hindu synthesis emerged after the Vedic period, between 500 BCE and 300 CE, in the period of the Second Urbanisation and the early classical period of Hinduism, when the Epics and the first Puranas were composed.

Jainism: A dualistic religion founded in the 6th century B.C. as a revolt against current Hinduism and emphasizing the perfectibility of human nature and liberation of the soul, especially through asceticism and nonviolence toward all living creatures.

To order more copies of this book, find books by other
Canadian authors, or make inquiries about publishing
your own book, contact PageMaster at:

PageMaster Publication Services Inc.
11340-120 Street, Edmonton, AB T5G 0W5
books@pagemaster.ca
780-425-9303

catalogue and e-commerce store
PageMasterPublishing.ca/Shop

About the author

My Name is Seyed Ali Asghar Emadi Pahandari, and I am an Iranian-Canadian. I came to Canada as a Marxist Leninist and later I found out I am not Marxist Leninist any more. I do not agree with any parties and organizations and I believe no party, organization or group can build a better world for people; thus, my book is a critic on Marx and Lenin. I do not agree with capitalism, but I think capitalism or imperialism must continue it a way until it reaches to better society.

I am against revolution and any kind of violence.

I believe any action that is going to be started in society must be started in imperialism, not in the capitalism society.

I believe we can reach perfection in a communist society that we cannot reach in class society. In communist society nobody has to lie, steal or murder anyone because everything a human needs, they have.

I hope this book help you to find out what is communist and how we can reach to this perfect society. Communist will not come until you are prepared for it.

Visit Ali's blog at https://tcommunist.blogspot.com/

cher d'entrer. En fait, les propriétaires n'étaient pas plus dérangés que ça par ceux qui voulaient un échantillon. On n'avait jamais faim. C'était entre la fin des années soixante et le début des années soixante-dix.

4

LA SILICON VALLEY

C'était le bazar dans le monde. Nous, on était dans la Guerre du Vietnam. J'ai vu tellement de mères pleurer en découvrant que leur fils avait été tué. Il y avait des enterrements au moins une fois par mois. On parlait beaucoup de la famille Manson aux infos. Il y a eu leur procès en direct à la télé, tous les jours. Patty Hearst et la *Symbionese Liberation Army* ont aussi fait les gros titres. Mais il y avait une chose, une seule, qui m'empêchait de dormir. Ma plus grande peur, quand j'allais au lit, c'était le Zodiac.

Mon père nous avait acheté un chien pour nous protéger. Il aboyait dès que quelqu'un passait devant la maison. Ça avait le don d'effrayer les enfants des voisins. C'était tellement marrant. Parfois, il décidait de se tailler par un trou dans la palissade. Il courait partout dans les champs.

On prenait toujours le chien avec nous quand on allait chasser. On essayait d'attraper des écureuils et des lapins. On n'avait pas de fusils, alors on faisait ce qu'on pouvait avec des roches. C'était pas évident et c'était un sacré défi. On arrivait à quelque chose environ une fois sur cent.

Chaque jour, on allait dans les champs et on jouait à suivre le guide. J'avais toujours des habits rouges. Un moment, j'avais des baskets noires avec une chemise à rayures bleues et blanches. C'est assez fou, aujourd'hui encore je peux fermer les yeux et revoir tout ça à nouveau. Il y avait un clochard sur la même piste que nous. Quelqu'un a crié « C'est le Zodiac! » On a tous crié et détalé en courant. On se dépassait l'un l'autre et on avait abandonné les filles derrière nous. J'étais tout petit et je courais aussi vite que possible avec mes jambes minuscules. Tous nos parents étaient sortis devant leur porche le temps qu'on arrive au trou dans la clôture. Tout le monde avait peur et avait cet air effrayé. La police est arrivée et a posé des questions à l'homme. Sans surprise, c'était juste un clochard. Mais on avait tous tellement peur.

Je me souviens de deux fois où je suis tombé en courant. Je pense que j'en porte encore les cicatrices sur mon genou. Je me souviens d'avoir couru vers ma mère en tremblant de peur. J'en avais rien à faire de qui me regardait devant l'immeuble. J'étais juste là, devant l'entrée, et je me suis pissé dessus. J'ai commencé à sucer mon pouce en tremblant. J'ai été traumatisé et je m'en suis jamais remis.

J'oublierai jamais ce jour-là. J'avais peur des fessées de mon père. Mais ça, c'était différent. C'était la première fois que je vivais de la véritable crainte. C'était quelque chose que je n'avais pas cherché, mais qui m'avait trouvé.

Mes parents ont déménagé deux mois plus tard à Sunnyvale. Notre nouvelle maison était à quatre maisons de la gare. Ce n'était plus un appartement, mais une maison en duplex. Le quartier était vraiment sympa. C'était comme déménager de « Mayberry » à « Leave it to beaver ». Tout ce qu'il y avait, c'était une poste, une station Greyhound et un Grissos Market qui vendait des têtes de porc.

5

LE ZODIAC

Vous savez comment il y a parfois une situation qui change votre vie pour toujours? Voilà la mienne: j'ai causé quelques problèmes en jouant avec un aiguillage à la gare. C'était l'anniversaire de Pam. Pam, c'était la sœur de Kathy, qui était elle-même ma copine. Mon frère, deux amis - Brian et Robin, Kathy et moi étions en train de boire. Pam a appelé et dit que sa mère viendrait chercher Kathy à Round Table Pizza parce que c'était l'anniversaire de Pam. Alors, on a marché jusqu'à Round Table Pizza, et traversé la gare jusqu'en ville et au centre commercial. En revenant, j'avais une bouteille de Black Velvet dans ma poche, qu'on avait bue avant.

Sorti de nulle part, sans qu'on ne lui ait rien fait, un mec a couru vers nous avec une machette à la main en criant « je vais vous couper les couilles ». Brian l'a poussé et on est parti de l'autre côté de la gare. Quand on est arrivé, tous les passagers avaient l'air effrayés. Il leur avait dit la même chose. On a essayé de rentrer par un raccourci avec un trou dans une palissade.

J'ai donné à Brian quelque chose à boire et on se passait la bouteille. On était assis à regarder le mec à la machette. J'étais en colère contre lui. Le même gars avait agressé un enfant. Tout ce qu'il voulait faire, l'enfant, c'était acheter le journal. Le gars disait que le distributeur de journaux devant la gare lui appartenait. On est reparti et on en a parlé à mon frère, vu que c'était le plus vieux. Il voulait rien n'y faire. Je me souviens de la peur que j'ai ressentie quand j'ai cru voir le Zodiac. C'était quelque chose que je ne ressentirai jamais à nouveau.

On a décidé de mettre le mec hors d'état de nuire. On a fumé un joint chez moi. Brian et moi sommes sortis et avons récupéré son fusil. C'était un fusil 22 LONG BARREL RIFLE. C'était un fusil à verrou un coup. Il l'appelait son « Fusil à Cerf. » Il a mis son viseur, l'a pointé dans la direction du fou et a dit « Je suis bon tireur. » J'avais changé d'avis, je me disais qu'on avait besoin de plus y réfléchir. Alors il a rangé le fusil et on est retourné chez moi.

On a fumé un autre joint et on est allé dans le garage. On a pris des battes de baseball et on est allé à la gare. On est passé par le trou dans la clôture. Mon frère nous suivait. En s'approchant, on essayait de cacher les battes dans notre dos. En arrivant, je lui ai lancé « Hé, monsieur, vous voulez toujours nous couper les couilles? » J'ai dit à Brian de le frapper en haut et que je le frapperais en bas. On l'a frappé comme il le fallait.

6

DOUZE ANS

Tabasser le sans-abri a changé ma vie. On s'est fait arrêter par la police de Sunnyvale. La police a retourné la maison pour nous trouver. Bernice et Harold, des amis un peu plus vieux de ma mère, savaient ce qu'il s'était passé et ont appelé les flics. Ils nous ont vu courir en pleine nuit avec nos habits ensanglantés. On s'est fait arrêter, mon frère a cafté. Il a tout raconté.

J'ai touché le fond à douze ans. J'étais totalement accro. Tout ce que je voulais faire, c'était me défoncer. J'allais plus à l'école. Je buvais toute la journée. Et maintenant, nouveauté... j'allais en prison. Mes parents ont divorcé peu de temps après l'incident à la gare. Je crois que ma mère a dit que c'était de la faute de mon père si j'étais devenu comme ça.

Mon frère a suivi mon père. Ma mère est restée seule. Jimmy ne m'a jamais dit pourquoi il avait choisi mon père. Je soupçonne que c'est parce que c'était lui qui avait l'argent et qu'il avait son entreprise.

Au tribunal, on a été rapidement condamnés à quatre ans et demi pour agression avec une arme létale. Ma carrière criminelle commençait.

7

LE CENTRE DE DÉTENTION POUR MINEURS

J'ai été envoyé à O.H. Close, une prison pour jeunes de la CYA (*California Youth Authority*) à Stockon. J'ai commencé la gym et le sport. C'était un programme qu'ils proposaient et je m'ennuyais. Après tout, j'étais toujours un enfant, et je n'avais que douze ans.

Je savais courir. J'ai concouru pour le cinquante et le cent mètres. J'étais le plus rapide en sprint 200 mètres et au relai. Je jouais aussi au foot, au volley et au basket. J'ai toujours le trophée du championnat KHS et celui du Holl Hall Basketball chez moi. Je me souviens que j'ai mis le panier gagnant depuis la ligne de faute. Je tirais du dessous, façon grand-mère, comme Rick Berry.

J'ai repris l'école dans le centre de détention pour mineurs. J'ai rapidement progressé, du General Education Diploma, je suis passé à une vraie classe pour avoir un diplôme du lycée. J'ai même terminé un programme d'université. J'ai un DEUG en sociologie. Et j'ai fait tout ça avant de franchir les dix-sept ans et demi.

On peut dire que l'État m'a élevé.

Ma copine Kathy est restée en contact pendant trois ans. J'avais des lettres et des photos d'elle tout le temps. Ça me faisait la manquer encore plus. C'était mon premier amour. Pendant tout mon premier séjour en prison, je n'ai jamais reçu aucune visite. Les personnes dont je pensais qu'elles m'aimaient et seraient là pour moi quoi qu'il arrive ne sont jamais venues, et j'espère ne garder aucun ressentiment dans mon cœur à ce sujet.

✖ ✖ ✖

Le jour est enfin arrivé pour moi de regagner ma vie et de sortir de prison. Étonnamment, ce ne fut pas ma mère, mais mon père, qui vint me chercher. Plutôt que de retourner à Sunnyvale, comme je l'imaginais, j'ai déménagé à Bangor (Californie) pour vivre avec mon père dans un bâtiment appartenant à mes grand-parents. C'était à cinquante kilomètres de la ville. Aller au cinéma, ou n'importe où, en fait, était une épopée. On vivait dans les champs et il y avait une dépendance pour les toilettes. La douche, c'était un tuyau d'arrosage. C'était... rustique, c'est le moins qu'on puisse dire. En fait, c'était même mieux en prison. Pourtant, c'était bien le dernier endroit où j'aurais voulu aller. Mon père allait tous les soirs au bar et revenait saoul. Il ramenait n'importe quelle fille qu'il trouvait. Le seul avantage, c'est que c'était vraiment calme. Mais quand ils faisaient l'amour, ça faisait de l'écho, et ça me faisait manquer ma copine.

J'ai fui, et je suis allé voir Kathy. Elle vivait à quelques pas de chez ma mère. Quand elle a ouvert la porte, je l'ai embrassée. On a déchiré nos vêtements et on a fait l'amour. Mais avant qu'on finisse, j'ai entendu un bébé pleurer dans la maison. Je lui ai demandé ce que c'était. Elle a répondu que c'était son enfant.

J'étais choqué, je voulais le voir. J'ai vu le bébé, et j'ai compris pourquoi ses lettres s'étaient faites plus rares.

En marchant en ville, j'ai vu Jimmy. Ça faisait quatre ans que je l'avais pas vu. Il avait pas changé, à part qu'il avait laissé pousser sa barbe. Il s'était marié, aussi. On a un peu parlé, et on est allé chez lui pour manger un morceau. Je suis parti et j'ai couru.

Quand j'ai revu Jimmy plus tard ce même jour, il était en colère. Il me dit que papa avait téléphoné et qu'il lui avait demandé s'il m'avait vu. Mon frère lui répondit que oui. J'ai dit à Jimmy de lui expliquer que je reviendrais bientôt mais que, pour l'heure, je revoyais d'anciens amis. Mon père était très en colère et dit à Jimmy que si je revenais pas maintenant, ça violait les conditions de ma liberté conditionnelle, ce qui voulait dire que je retournerais en prison. C'était vraiment la dernière chose dont j'avais envie, alors je suis rentré contre mon gré. J'ai acheté un ticket de car et j'ai repris le long voyage vers Hicksville.

Ma philosophie de vie est devenue « Si tu peux pas les battre, rejoins-les. » Je me suis inscrit à l'université de Butte et j'ai commencé les cours de psychologie. Je me suis mis à traîner sur le campus. Il y avait plus de gens de mon âge. J'ai rencontré des filles plutôt mignonnes qui aimaient boire et faire la fête et j'en ai choisi une pour copine.

Un peu plus tard, j'ai découvert que son frère faisait de la meth. Son frère et moi sommes devenus amis et il m'a rapidement introduit au marché. J'ai appris à fabriquer de la méthamphétamine et maintenant je pouvais être défoncé gratuitement.

8

ANGIE

J'étais devenu un « cuisinier » et je gagnais ma vie. J'ai appris à ne pas avoir peur en cuisinant. C'était comme ça que les gens explosaient ou brûlaient. J'ai fait ça pendant un temps, mais la drogue se répandait vite et était sans pitié. Chaque jour, des gens mouraient à cause de ça.

Ma relation s'est améliorée avec une fille que je voyais. Elle était mon meilleur espoir en matière de vie normale. Je n'avais jamais connu l'Amour de ma vie, alors j'ai admis que c'était elle. Alors je me suis marié avec Angie. C'était mon ange. Elle ne prenait pas de drogue, et elle ne buvait que du vin. J'avais vingt-cinq ans; c'était maintenant ou jamais.

En me baladant un jour, je me suis fait ramasser. J'étais toujours en liberté conditionnelle. J'avais peur de retourner en prison. J'ai avoué mon amour à Angie, et on s'est marié au téléphone. Le prêtre était sur un téléphone et elle sur un autre. C'était fou. J'avais un téléphone à chaque oreille. La cérémonie a duré environ cinq minutes. Elle avait apporté une alliance. Un flic m'a donné la bague à la fin du mariage. Quand je suis retourné au tribunal, le juge a dit « Oh, vous êtes marié. Allez-y et consommez votre mariage. » Il a suspendu ma sentence et m'a dit de rentrer chez moi et d'être un brave homme.

On a essayé de s'installer et de vivre une vie normale mais elle voulait contrôler ma vie. Je me suis mis à boire et à fumer pour gérer le stress. Ça avait pas fait long feu : trois ans après nos vœux, j'étais à nouveau dealer de meth. C'était principalement dû au fait que j'avais pas d'argent, et qu'elle pouvait pas s'empêcher de me le rappeler. Je savais que dealer de la meth était un boulot facile et que ça rapportait. J'ai dit à mon épouse qu'elle n'avait plus à se soucier de son salaire. Angie a adoré cette nouvelle source de revenus. Elle achetait tout ce qu'elle voulait, et avec mon argent. J'entendais pas de reproches en rentrant.

Plus je m'enfonçais dans le milieu, moins on parlait. Je restais loin de la maison pendant de longs jours. Quand elle me voyait, elle se faisait du souci pour ma santé. Elle voulait que je reste à la maison, mais j'avais pas envie de l'écouter.

Après un bout de temps, j'ai réalisé que j'étais à nouveau accro et j'ai décidé de partir en cure de désintox. À l'époque, c'était devenu normal pour moi de rester debout pendant des semaines. La désintox, c'était un peu comme un espoir auquel se raccrocher. En plus, c'était pris en charge par nos mutuelles. Mon patron savait que je buvais au travail et était d'accord pour me laisser y aller.

La cure n'a duré que seize jours. J'avais l'impression que tout allait bien. Et puis j'ai vu Pam, une amie d'Angie. Ce fut la seule visite que j'ai eue là-bas. Je l'ai regardé venir dans le hall et j'ai souri. Elle faisait une tête un peu étrange. Je lui ai demandé « Qu'est-ce qu'il se passe, Pam? » Elle n'a rien répondu, et m'a tendu une grande enveloppe. C'était les papiers pour le divorce.

J'ai regardé à travers la fenêtre et j'ai vu Angie dans une voiture. J'ai levé mes bras au ciel, incompréhensif. Elle est venue, et elle m'a dit qu'elle n'avait pas envie de divorcer, mais que c'était ce qu'on lui avait conseillé de faire. Tout le monde disait qu'il fallait que je me concentre sur moi-même. Alors j'ai dit d'accord, et j'ai signé les papiers.

C'était pas la seule mauvaise nouvelle que j'aie eue pendant la cure de désintoxication. La maison que mes grand-parents avaient construite avait brûlé dans un incendie. Ma grand-mère s'était échappée, mais mon grand-père n'avait pas réussi à sortir à temps. Elle me raconta l'incident. Elle me dit qu'elle l'avait vu en flammes et qu'il était tombé devant la porte d'entrée, en essayant de sortir. Il lui avait sauvé la vie. Les voisins, eux, avaient tenté de sauver la maison, mais elle avait été mise en cendres avant que toute vraie aide puisse arriver. Mon grand-père perdit la vie ce jour-là.

Je me demande toujours si les choses avaient été différentes, si j'avais été là. Mon grand-père avait disparu. Je n'avais pas le droit d'assister aux funérailles. Les responsables disaient que c'en serait trop pour un début de désintoxication. Ça me faisait tellement mal de pas pouvoir être là. J'essayais d'aller mieux, mais je ne pouvais pas me concentrer sur quoi que ce soit.

Rapidement, je me suis mis à aller mieux, et à me demander ce que j'allais faire. Ma famille ne voulait plus de moi, de peur que je me remette à faire de la meth. Ils m'ont dit que les Alcohol, Tobacco and Firearms et la DEA étaient partout, et qu'il y avait des explosions de labos à meth toutes les semaines. Je ne comprenais pas trop ce qu'ils faisaient mal, mais ça avait rendu les endroits où on avait cuisiné difficiles. On pouvait entendre les hélicoptères et la police en véhicules tous-terrains rouler à travers les champs toute la journée. Je savais que faire de la meth était un crime, mais qu'est-ce que je pouvais faire? Et où est ce que je pouvais aller? En fait, la meth avait été mon seul gagne-pain. Il se passait trop de choses dans ma vie et dans ma tête. Je suis resté loin des collines, mais je ne savais toujours pas quoi faire.

Et puis, tout a changé: un ami m'a fait essayer l'héroïne.

9

L'HÉROÏNE

L'héroïne envoie une grande sensation de chaud dans le corps. Quand j'en prenais, je me sentais invisible. Au début, ça me faisait du bien; sur le long terme, je sentais que ça me faisait beaucoup de mal. Plus j'en prenais, plus j'en voulais. Je remplissais les seringues et je m'injectais tout. Le problème avec l'héroïne, c'est qu'on sait pas trop ce que c'est et avec quoi c'est coupé. Au moins, quand je prenais de la meth, je savais ce qu'il y avait dedans.

Parfois, je mettais la main sur un peu de très bonne héroïne. Le reste du temps... c'était moins bien. J'ai sacrément mis ma vie en danger. J'ai fait trois overdoses. À chaque fois, j'étais plus téméraire. Quelques connaissances en sont mortes. J'avais bien conscience que je courais droit à ma perte moi aussi. Comme j'avais besoin d'aide, je suis parti dans un centre de désintoxication en centre-ville. Je savais que je finirais par me tuer si je le faisais pas.

C'était une clinique temporaire. On pouvait partir quand on voulait. Là-bas, j'ai croisé un ancien pote qui tentait aussi de se remettre dans le droit chemin. J'ai cuisiné de la meth avec lui dans les collines. Il en avait marre de la cure et m'a demandé si je voulais partir. J'étais presque arrivé à rompre l'addiction, c'était horrible. Ils me donnaient souvent de la méthadone pour faire partir les crises. Ca marchait bien au début, mais mon corps voulait toujours de l'héroïne. Je savais que je devais rester clean. Lui, il voulait vraiment partir, et il voulait absolument que je parte avec lui. J'étais, genre, à quoi bon partir si de toute façon t'es fauché? Il m'a dit qu'il avait un peu de drogue et d'argent enterrés. J'avais pas besoin d'en entendre plus, et on s'est tiré.

J'ai recommencé à vendre de la drogue, mais cette fois je me suis tenu loin de l'héroïne. J'arrivais pas à me contrôler avec elle. Avec le speed, je choisissais quand j'en voulais. L'héroïne, il fallait que j'en prenne pour me sentir normal. Ca fait partie des démons dont j'étais heureux de me débarrasser.

10

RENDEZ-VOUS

Je faisais des progrès, et j'ai recommencé à sortir avec des femmes. J'ai rencontré cette jolie norvégienne. Elle était professeure de yoga. Elle était toute petite, un mètre cinquante, et pesait pas plus de cinquante kilos. C'était une vraie blonde avec des yeux clairs. Tout en elle m'excitait. Elle avait une incroyable personnalité.

On a rapidement développé une relation forte. Emménager avec elle était la meilleure décision de ma vie. Enfin, c'est ce que je pensais.

Un jour, elle a trouvé ma réserve. J'étais un utilisateur classique, je me défonçais et je cachais mes trucs partout. Il y avait du speed partout dans l'appartement. Elle aussi, en fait. Quand je dormais, elle cherchait mes réserves et se servait.

Un jour, j'ai perdu conscience dans la baignoire. J'avais pas dormi pendant huit jours, à faire la fête. C'était pas grand-chose, pour moi. J'ai encore du mal à croire ce qu'elle m'a fait. Je serais incapable de dire si j'avais fait quelque chose ou si c'était juste la drogue qui l'avait rendue folle.

Elle a mis des clous en dessous du tapis de la salle de bain pendant que j'étais inconscient. Elle a aussi mis de l'insecticide partout dans la salle de bain pendant que j'étais dans la baignoire. La jolie fille que j'aimais tant essayait de me tuer.

Elle avait des serviettes scotchées à ses pieds pour ne pas se blesser. Et elle gazait notre appartement. Je me suis réveillé parce que l'eau était devenue froide. En sortant de la baignoire, j'ai ressenti une douleur intense dans mon pied. J'avais marché sur un clou. J'ai commencé à tousser dans les vapeurs. Je sentais le poison dans la maison. Je l'ai vue, debout dans le cadre de la porte. Elle cria « J'ai essayé de te prévenir! ». J'ai couru et je lui ai arraché la bombe des mains. J'ai ouvert une fenêtre, y ai jeté la bombe, et j'ai ouvert tout ce qui pouvait l'être.

J'ai mis une serviette autour de ma tête pour arrêter les vapeurs. Je l'ai tenue dans mes bras et elle a commencé à pleurer. Je lui ai demandé si elle allait bien. Tout ce qu'elle arrivait à faire était d'acquiescer en disant « oui ». Je me suis habillé, j'ai attrapé tout le matériel et la drogue, lui ai donné deux mille dollars, et je suis parti.

J'ai tout déposé chez un ami. J'avais besoin d'aller consulter pour connaître l'état de mon pied. Je suis allé aux urgences, ça a pris du temps, mais j'ai eu droit à une consultation. Il m'a fait une piqûre d'antibiotiques à la fesse et a dit que tout irait bien puisque je n'avais que très peu été exposé au spray. Quand je lui ai raconté l'histoire de ma copine norvégienne qui voulait m'empoisonner, elle a ri. J'ai cru qu'elle allait appeler la police. Je pense qu'elle me croyait pas.

J'ai jamais appelé les flics. Je voulais pas les savoir impliqués là-dedans. J'ai horreur des flics. Mais j'ai pris ce signe comme un avertissement que cette femme était empoisonnée, et je ne l'ai jamais revue.

✖ ✖ ✖

Après ça, j'ai eu un autre accident avec une copine. Elle a commencé à traîner avec des suprémacistes. Un jour, elle m'a dit qu'ils voulaient acheter du speed. Ils étaient dans ma zone, mais ils étaient vraiment dangereux. Au début, j'avais des doutes quant à l'idée de leur vendre des choses. Ils nous mettaient des colis à récupérer, à déposer ou de l'argent à collecter. Je me souviens qu'une fois, un ami à moi a été exécuté. Il avait été accusé de diluer le produit. Ils s'y sont tous mis. Ils se sont arrêtés au bord d'une route vide, ils l'ont sorti de la voiture, lui ont bandé les yeux et l'ont couché. Ils se sont baissés et lui ont tiré une balle dans la tête.

J'avais pas envie de mourir. Quand j'ai appris pour l'exécution, j'ai commencé à faire comme si j'étais sous acide. Je disais n'importe quoi et je faisais comme si j'en étais plus. Je faisais plein de trucs bizarres genre leur demander s'ils voyaient toutes les lignes. Le jour d'après, j'ai continué en leur demandant « au fait, vous m'en avez donné combien ? J'arrive pas à me souvenir de rien. » Juste après, j'ai quitté la ville.

11

SOBRE

J'ai été sobre pendant deux ans. La vie était plutôt belle. J'avais quarante-six ans, je vivais à Gilroy. J'avais une pension d'invalidité de la Sécurité Sociale. C'était juste assez d'argent pour payer mes factures et avoir un peu d'argent en plus chaque mois. J'avais droit à ça parce que j'avais été alcoolique et drogué. Je dédiais la majorité de mon temps libre aux rencontres des Narcotiques Anonymes. J'avais même mes propres réunions. J'étais même parrain de certains. Les réunions avaient lieu dans une ancienne caserne de pompiers à Gilroy. Maintenant, c'est un Station 55.

Un jour, cette fille arrive par la porte comme une bouffée d'air frais. Je pouvais pas m'empêcher de la regarder. Norman, un membre des NA, m'a dit « Non, pas elle. » J'ai rigolé et je suis parti.

Après la réunion, je lui ai donné mon numéro et on a commencé à parler. Elle avait l'air plutôt bien. On a commencé à se voir en dehors des réunions pour parler et fumer des cigarettes. On avait tellement d'expériences communes. Nos conversations étaient sans limites. On allait manger des sushis et prendre des petits-déjeuners.

Un jour, je suis allé la chercher chez elle et elle était saoule. Je lui ai demandé ce qu'il se passait, elle m'a parlé de son mari et de sa famille. Elle était aussi en colère parce qu'elle avait dû revenir à Gilroy. Je lui ai dit que j'allais l'aider. Elle m'a donné quatre cents dollars et je l'ai aidée à déménager.

Après l'avoir réemménagé chez sa mère, j'ai demandé aux autres femmes du programme d'aller la chercher et de l'amener aux réunions. J'essayais de l'encourager à arrêter de boire. À l'époque, on sortait ensemble depuis six mois. Elle commençait à redevenir sobre. Un jour, elle m'a dit qu'elle avait besoin de quelqu'un pour aller dans un motel avec elle parce que sa mère l'avait jetée dehors. Alors je suis resté avec elle au motel.

Vivre avec elle dans le motel était plutôt cool. Il n'y avait que ses règles à respecter, et c'était d'être là toutes les nuits. J'ai emménagé avec elle et arrêté de vivre à la *sober house*.

Après six mois, j'ai décidé de boire un verre. C'était une bouteille de tequila. Boire m'a impliqué dans d'autres choses.

J'ai vu certains de mes anciens amis, et j'ai replongé dans le milieu de la drogue. On allait de motel en motel, ça a duré deux ans. Elle a appelé sa mère et m'a dénoncé. Sa mère et moi étions devenus proches avec le temps. Sa mère a envoyé un de ses fils au motel pour essayer de me convaincre de devenir sobre à nouveau. J'ai été sobre une semaine, et j'ai replongé. J'imagine que c'est ma personnalité, d'être accro comme ça. Le frère m'a averti de quelques trucs sombres dans lesquels sa sœur était impliquée. Il m'a dit de l'abandonner. Que quelqu'un pourrait très bien venir la tuer au motel. Je lui ai dit que ça n'arriverait pas avec moi.

Elle m'a menti un jour et appelé les flics. Elle voulait juste se venger parce que j'avais pris de la drogue. Elle pensait peut-être que ça me rendrait clean à nouveau. À l'époque, j'étais dans le trafic et un ami m'avait prévenu que la police m'attendait au motel. Quand je lui ai demandé ce qu'il se passait, il m'a dit qu'il y avait une prime de cinquante mille dollars sur ma tête pour violences conjugales. Je tombais des nues. Je ne l'avais jamais touchée.

Je me suis fait arrêter un jour sur la Monterey Highway. Un sheriff qui passait par là décida de m'enfermer. J'ai pu sortir et j'ai eu un ordre d'éloignement, je devais rester loin d'elle. J'ai ignoré le papier. J'étais sûr que c'était pas un vrai ordre d'éloignement issu d'un tribunal.

Je n'avais nulle part où vivre. Elle m'a appelé, elle se demandait ce que je faisais. J'ai accepté d'aller la voir. Elle m'a donné sa carte bancaire et m'a dit d'aller acheter une bouteille d'alcool. Je lui en ai pris deux, et trois pour moi. Je lui ai acheté la vodka qu'elle aime et du whisky pour moi. J'ai aussi acheté deux cartouches de cigarettes.

On a fait la fête toute la nuit, ou presque. Juste après, on se disputait. Je suis sorti pour me calmer et fumer une cigarette. J'avais bu deux cinquièmes et j'étais ivre mort. Je lui en voulais toujours pour ce qu'elle avait dit. Il y avait quelques personnes dehors. Ils vaquaient à leurs occupations, j'ai pas fait attention. Elle est sortie et m'a vu. Il y avait un mec avec ses potes. Ils ont vu ma belle. Il a dit « Comment ça va, ma belle ? » J'ai crié que c'était la mienne. Il m'a dit de me mêler de mes affaires. On aurait dit qu'elle l'avait poussé à le dire. En moins de deux, on était en train de se battre au milieu de la rue. Je crois qu'elle essayait de s'interposer, je l'ai giflée. Et après ça, je me souviens plus.

Quand je me suis réveillé, j'étais mort. Elle aussi était morte. On était apparemment retourné dans notre chambre. Sa tête était dans un sale état. Elle saignait pas mais elle avait l'air très mal. Le côté gauche de ma voiture était totalement noir. Je lui demandai ce qu'il s'était passé, elle est juste partie. Le manager l'a vue et lui a dit de s'asseoir un peu. J'imagine qu'on avait été cambriolés, vu notre état. Ils ont appelé les flics et l'ambulance. Je me suis cassé. Des amis mon récupéré au Walmart. Ils m'ont amené chez un autre pote pour désaouler. Il m'a dit que j'allais retourner en désintox mais que d'abord j'allais passer par l'hôpital pour ma tête. J'en pouvais plus. Quand je me suis enregistré aux urgences, j'ai remarqué que le personnel sortait plein de gens. Des officiers m'ont couru dessus. J'étais en train de me faire arrêter.

✖ ✖ ✖

Ils m'ont condamné pour violences conjugales. Aucun garant de caution ne voulait de moi. On m'a dit que j'en avais pour trois ans et demi sans possibilité de libération. J'ai demandé ce que j'avais fait, et qui était la victime. Je n'avais aucun souvenir. Le blackout total. Ils en avaient rien à faire, on m'a dit de poser la question au juge.

On m'a collé un avocat commis d'office. Pendant la première écoute, les accusations se sont transformées en blessures aggravées et tentative de meurtre. Ça changeait pas mal. La peine aussi changeait pas mal: je risquais de sept ans à perpétuité. J'étais, genre, qu'est-ce qu'il s'est passé ? On m'a dit qu'elle avait été frappée et qu'elle était méconnaissable. Que son pronostic vital était engagé à cause des blessures au cerveau.

Elle est venue à la première session et a témoigné contre moi. Elle a raconté une histoire horrible, je l'avais agressée et battue.

J'étais choqué. Choqué de voir que quelqu'un dont j'étais devenu si proche puisse inventer et dire une histoire pareille. Peut-être que je lui avais fait ces choses, cette nuit-là. Dieu seul sait ce qu'il s'est vraiment passé.

L'avocat m'a dit que le procureur de la République proposait sept ans à 85%. Plaider non-coupable me promettait une peine sans perpétuité alors j'ai sauté sur l'occasion.

En prison, elle m'a envoyé une lettre, pour me dire qu'elle était désolée.

La prison dans laquelle j'étais était dure. Non seulement il fallait se méfier des autres détenus, mais aussi des gardes. J'étais seul dans ma cellule, j'avais pas à me préoccuper des autres. Mais il y avait d'horribles surveillants. Ils donnaient des ordres à tout le monde et battaient ceux qui n'obéissaient pas.

Un jour, en revenant du tribunal, j'ai demandé à parler au département pour la santé mentale. Le tribunal et la sentence qu'ils voulaient prononcer commençaient à être un peu trop longs. J'étais en train de perdre le peu de raison qui me restait. L'infirmière appela les gardes. Deux officiers sont venus dans ma cellule et m'ont frappé. Ils m'ont menotté et mené à une salle d'interview. Quand les responsables de la santé mentale sont venus m'interviewer, je leur ai dit que les flics essayaient de me tuer. Un officier a regardé la dame de la santé mentale et lui a demandé quoi faire. Elle m'avait déjà vu dans le passé et ne m'avait jamais vu comme ça. Elle choisit d'appeler son supérieur pour prendre une décision.

J'étais maintenant tout seul dans la salle. J'avais peur, parce que je savais de quoi les officiers étaient capables. Ils m'ont désha-billé et m'ont enchaîné. J'ai été emmené dans une pièce, on m'a donné une tunique anti-suicide et on m'a placé sous surveillance. Je voulais pas.

Pendant qu'ils m'emmenaient à la salle cadenassée, ils m'ont détruit le bras. J'arrêtais pas de taper sur la porte et de crier à l'aide en demandant un médecin. Un officier est venu, m'a regardé et a dit que mon bras avait l'air en bonne santé. Il m'a prévenu: il fallait se taire, sinon ils reviendraient pour me frapper. J'ai continué et ils sont revenus. Cette fois, ils m'ont tabassé jusqu'à ce que je m'évanouisse.

J'ai finalement pu consulter un médecin. Mon bras n'était pas cassé. Par contre, les officiers qui m'ont agressé sont actuellement assis dans le centre de réception de San Quentin pour avoir tué un détenu qui refusait de prendre ses médicaments.

12

FIN

Je suis sobre depuis sept ans. J'attends d'être libéré. J'ai quelques problèmes de santé, mais à part ça, je suis prêt à trouver une femme et à m'installer. J'ai juste envie d'aller en croisière et de me détendre, de jouer au bingo et aux palets. J'ai juste envie de vivre. J'ai déjà passé trop d'années en prison. J'ai déjà passé trop d'années à chercher la drogue. Je me suis réveillé un jour et je me suis dit que cette vie, faite de prison et de drogue n'est pas la mienne. Je vaux mieux que ça. Je suis maintenant Bouddhiste. Je suis laïque, mais ça me donne des lignes de conduite à suivre. Je me suis converti, et j'espère que ça me gardera loin de la drogue. J'ai vraiment hâte de voir ce que ça donne.

EAST OAKLAND TIMES, LLC

Le *East Oakland Times, LLC* (EOT) est une publication multi-média de la baie de San Francisco. Fondée par son rédacteur en chef, Tio MacDonald, il tient deux principes à cœur: le respect de la vie et la liberté. EOT soutient le développement et l'épanouissement de l'humanité à travers la paix. La paix ne saura être trouvée que lorsque la vie et la liberté seront respectées et honorées.

Parmi les projets actuels de l'East Oakland Times, on retrouve:

- La série My Crime;
- La publication de contenu original (œuvres d'art et livres) de détenus;
- Des podcasts concernant le Couloir de la Mort en Californie;
- Des impressions trimestrielles distribuées gratuitement dans les rues de East Oaklan ;
- Un site Internet où les détenus peuvent donner des informations sur les événements en cours.

En laissant un commentaire positif sur ce livre, vous incitez les autres à le lire également et ainsi, vous soutenez la mission de l'EOT.

Pour des bonus uniques, notamment des interviews audio de Jay Jay enregistrées à la prison de San Quentin, rendez-vous sur www.crimebios.com

Soutenez l'EOT en vous procurant ses livres, ses e-books et ses livres audio!

Gardez un esprit libre et heureux!

Soyez et restez béni!

Faites le bien autour de vous!

Tio MacDonald

East Oakland Times

Fondateur et rédacteur en chef

EAST
OAKLAND

www.ingramcontent.com/pod-product-compliance
Lightning Source LLC
Chambersburg PA
CBHW060655280326
41933CB00012B/2192